don't blame the mud

ONLY JESUS MAKES US CLEAN

WRITTEN BY
Marty Machowski
ILLUSTRATED BY
Craig MacIntosh

New Growth Press, Greensboro, NC 27404
www.newgrowthpress.com
Copyright © 2019 by Marty Machowski
Illustration copyright © 2019 by New Growth Press

Cover Design, Interior Design, and Typesetting: Trish Mahoney, themahoney.com
Cover and Interior Illustrations by Craig MacIntosh

ISBN: 978-1-948130-96-7

Library of Congress Cataloging-in-Publication Data

Names: Machowski, Martin, 1963- author.
Title: Don't blame the mud : only Jesus makes us clean / Marty Machowski.
Description: Greensboro : New Growth Press, 2019.
Identifiers: LCCN 2018060559 | ISBN 9781948130967 (trade cloth)
Subjects: LCSH: Sin--Christianity--Juvenile literature. |
  Sin--Christianity--Study and teaching. | Christian education of children.
Classification: LCC BT715 .M1275 2019 | DDC 242/.62--dc23
LC record available at https://lccn.loc.gov/2018060559

Printed in Malaysia

26 25 24 23 22 21 20 19   1 2 3 4 5

For God so loved the world, that he gave his only Son,
that whoever believes in him should not perish but have eternal life.

JOHN 3:16

My troubles began one spring day as I was walking home from school. The rain had stopped, and the sun was shining.

As I jumped over mud puddles, I could hear my mom's parting words echoing in my head: **"Max! Don't get those clothes dirty! Come home and change before you play."**

I looked down at my new school uniform—it was still clean. *Whew!*

I should have kept walking down the sidewalk, but the trail that ran along the creek looked so much more fun. The muddy path seemed to call out to me that day. *I can keep my clothes clean,* I thought, *and I can catch frogs and skip stones.* Soon I forgot all about Mom's warning.

I walked on logs.
I hopped from rock to rock
over puddles and patches of mud.
I dodged the mud splashes.

"Missed me,"
I shouted as I ducked a huge one.
Mom will never know I came home this way, I thought. Then, all of a sudden, a frog jumped across the path.

I ran after the frog,
but tripped on a stick.

I grabbed hold of a tree branch.
I hung on tight.
The branch broke my fall
and swung me over to a mossy log.

That was a close call, I thought as I let go of the branch.
It sprang back into place, far back on the other side of a sea of mud.

Now, I was trapped.

Everywhere I turned, the mud blocked my way. My only hope was to make it to a large flat rock in the middle of the muck. I backed down the log to get a good start. Then I took off and ran. But just as I jumped, my foot slid and slipped. I missed the rock, fell toward the mud, and this time there were no branches to save me.

When I hit the mud, it made a huge splash.
The cold slime soaked through to my skin.

"Oh no!" I shouted as I sprang
to my feet to try to get out of the mud.
As I stood, I heard Mom's voice
calling for me from up on the road.

"Max, where are you?" she shouted.
I'm in big trouble, I thought.

I shook the mud from my hands and stomped my feet on the path, but there was no way to get rid of that mud. It clung to my pants and my shirt and my socks and my shoes. The mud smelled worse than dead fish.

Now what am I going to do? I wondered
as Mom walked down the road.
She was still calling for me.
*I must get out of these clothes before
Mom finds out*, I thought.

So, I scrambled up the steps to my house.
I went in through the back door
and snuck up to my room.

I made it! Whew!

I kicked off my shoes and took off my muddy clothes. I wiped my face on my shirt. I threw on clean clothes as fast as I could and stuffed the smelly uniform under my bed.

It's not my fault, I thought.
I was doing fine till I slipped and fell.
My clothes were all clean
till the mud splashed on me.

It's all the mud's fault, that's easy to see.

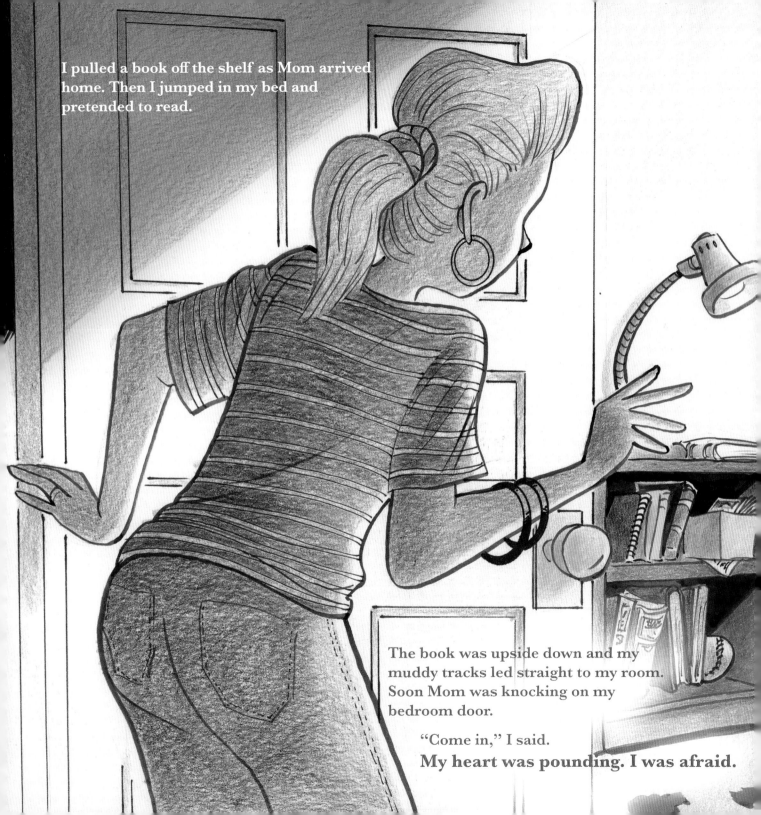

I pulled a book off the shelf as Mom arrived home. Then I jumped in my bed and pretended to read.

The book was upside down and my muddy tracks led straight to my room. Soon Mom was knocking on my bedroom door.

"Come in," I said.

My heart was pounding. I was afraid.

"Max," she said, "don't try to fool me. You tracked mud through the kitchen and down the hall. The footprints lead right to your room."

I slowly lowered the book and looked around. My dirty clothes were peeking out from under the bed. There was mud everywhere. It seemed to be laughing at me.

"Get your muddy uniform out from under your bed," Mom ordered. "Toss it into the washer then go take a shower. We'll talk after you're clean." I didn't say a word as I pulled out the ball of clothes. The mud on my pants and my shirt shouted one word: **guilty**.

Once in the bathroom, the mirror revealed a swipe of mud on my cheek and a clod in my hair. I had mud on my neck, my shoulders, and my chest.

"No wonder she figured it out," I said. Then I jumped in the shower to scrub it away.

After my shower, I still didn't feel clean. Somewhere down deep inside, the mud seemed to stay. I put on clean clothes and slowly walked down the hall.

"Max," my dad called.
"Come into the living room."
As I turned the corner I saw him
standing with Mom, holding my
muddy shoes. "What happened
today?" he asked.

I took a deep breath and tried to explain.
"It's not my fault that I slipped and fell.
My clothes were clean till the mud splashed me.
It's the mud's fault. It wasn't me."

Dad shook his head and said, "Max, try that again. This time don't blame the mud. Mom reminded you when you left for the day not to get dirty. You have no one to blame but yourself."

I knew Dad was right.
I was to blame. I lowered my
head. Mom put her arm around
me as I spoke through my tears.

"I showered and scrubbed till
the mud was all gone. But down
deep it still feels like it's there."

"Max," my mom said as she looked into my eyes, "the mud you still feel is guilt because you didn't obey. God says that we all try to go our own way, not God's way. That's what sin is. We think doing what we want will make us happy, but instead we feel sad and bad inside. Only God can wash away the mud in our hearts."

Dad went on to explain, "We all are born with the stain of sin, so we all disobey. That's why God sent his Son Jesus to die on the cross in our place.

If you turn from your own way—your sin—and believe in Jesus, your sin and guilt will be washed away. And God will give you a new, clean heart and his Spirit to help you turn from sin and go God's way."

I had heard the story of Jesus a hundred times. But there in that moment, God helped me see that Jesus died on the cross for ME and only he can make me clean!

Deep down inside I knew it was true and that God was calling me to turn from my sin and trust in Jesus. So I closed my eyes and began talking to God.

"God, I disobeyed Mom and lied to my dad," I confessed. "I believe you sent Jesus to die for my sins. I scrubbed off the mud. It went down the drain. But deep in my heart the stain still remains. Please forgive me."

Right there in a flash, God turned my sadness to joy. God forgave all of my sins and washed me clean. I felt brand-new inside. My sad tears gave way to a big smile.

Then I told my parents the true story. They heard all my sins and forgave every one. They both gave me a hug. The worst day turned into the best day. **Whew!**

The mud was all gone and so was my shame. My heart was washed clean, and deep inside I knew God was now living with me.

HELPING YOUR CHILD UNDERSTAND SIN

Sin is a short word the Bible uses to describe how we turn away from God and go our own way. We sin when we turn away from what God tells us to do in his Word and instead do what we want. After we sin, we blame others and say things like; "You made me angry!" and "It's all your fault." Or even blame the mud like Max did. But other people can't make us sin. The sin in our lives comes from our hearts.

Sin began a long time ago when Adam and Eve decided to not trust in God's love for them and instead listened to another voice—the voice of the Serpent. So they disobeyed God and ate the fruit God told them not to eat. Just like we inherit our eye color from our parents, we inherit from Adam and Eve wanting to go our way and not God's way. Did you ever wonder why wanting our own way comes naturally to everyone? It's because we take after our parents, grandparents, great-grandparents, and all the way back to Adam and Eve. We are born sinners.

The Bible tells us that sin begins in our hearts when we are tempted to go our way, not God's way (James 1:14). That's what happened to Max. He got the idea to take the muddy path through the woods. His mom said no. But doing what he wanted seemed so much more fun than listening. The moment we decide to act on a sinful idea (temptation), sin is born in our heart.

The Bible tells us our sin leads to death (James 1:15). That doesn't mean that we only die physically; it also means that sin brings every bad thing into our world—meanness, lies, stealing—it all starts with wanting our own way.

We can be tempted by even good things like ice cream and candy if we love them more than God. Max loved the fun of playing in the woods more than he loved God who said, "Children, obey your parents" (Ephesians 6:1). Max chose the muddy path rather than obeying his mom.

ASK YOUR CHILD:

Can you think of a time when you were tempted to do something wrong and disobeyed like Max?
Can you think of a time when you blamed someone or something for your sin?
How did you feel when you did something wrong?
Did you ever feel like Max?

HELPING YOUR CHILD UNDERSTAND THE GOSPEL

Long before the world began, God knew Adam and Eve would disobey him and bring sin into the world. God also knew that Adam and Eve couldn't save themselves and once they passed on their sin to their children, everyone everywhere would sin. So, God came up with a plan to rescue us from sin. We call his plan, "the gospel." The word *gospel* means "good news." The good news is this: God sent his only Son Jesus to save us from our sin. Jesus left his throne in heaven to come to earth to be born a man and break the curse of sin. To break the curse of sin, Jesus had to first live a perfect life and then die on the cross to take our blame.

Jesus lived his whole life without ever turning away from God the Father or doing anything wrong. Jesus healed the sick and opened the eyes of the blind and called all people to turn away from sin and believe in him. A few people followed Jesus and believed, but others did not believe. They told lies about Jesus and said he disobeyed God. The people Jesus came to save nailed him to a cross to kill him. Jesus was the only person ever who didn't have to die for his own sins. He never thought, said, or did anything wrong. Because he didn't deserve to die, he could take our place.

Because God the Father's plan was to send Jesus to rescue his people, he did not rescue Jesus as he died on the cross. There on the cross, Jesus paid for the sins of all who believe in him. We deserve death for our sins, but Jesus died in our place. When we trust in Jesus, God washes away all our sin and gives us the perfect sinless record of his Son. The proof that this is true is that Jesus rose from the dead, and because he lives forever, we know we will live forever too. God the Father adopts us into his family and sends his Spirit to live in our hearts to help us love Jesus and live for him. Instead of being like Adam and Eve, with the help of the Spirit, we can grow to be like Jesus. God's Spirit living in us is another proof we have that one day God will welcome us along with all of his children into heaven.

ASK YOUR CHILD:

What about you? Will you turn away from your sin and trust in Jesus to wash your sin away?

Here are five simple steps you can take:

1. **Repent** Turn away from your sin.
2. **Confess** Admit your sins to God and pray to ask him to forgive you.
3. **Believe** Place your trust in Jesus and his work on the cross to die in your place.
4. **Share** Tell others that you are trusting in Jesus to wash away your sins.
5. **Follow** Obey the words of Jesus in the Bible and live for him the rest of your life.

KEY BIBLE VERSES TO REMEMBER

A PROMISE:

If we walk in the light, as he is in the light,
we have fellowship with one another,
and the blood of Jesus his Son cleanses us from all sin.
If we say we have no sin, we deceive ourselves,
and the truth is not in us.
If we confess our sins,
he is faithful and just to forgive us our sins
and to cleanse us from all unrighteousness.

(1 JOHN 1:7–9)

A PRAYER:

Have mercy on me, O God,
according to your unfailing love;
according to your great compassion
blot out my transgressions.
Wash away all my iniquity
and cleanse me from my sin.

(PSALM 51:1–2 NIV)

A PLEA:

Jesus said:
"If I do not wash you,
you have no share with me."

(JOHN 13:8)